Arnold Schwarzenegger

Hard Work Brought Success

Christopher Meeks

illustrated by Teri Rider

The Rourke Corporation, Inc.   Vero Beach, Florida

© 1993 by The Rourke Corporation, Inc.

The Rourke Corporation, Inc.
P.O. Box 3328, Vero Beach, FL 32964

Series Editor: Gregory Lee
Production: The Creative Spark, San Clemente, CA
Illustration Design: Lee Ann Leigh

Library of Congress Cataloging-in-Publication Data

Meeks, Christopher.
    Arnold Schwarzenegger, hard work brought success / by
Christopher Meeks.
            p. cm. — (Reaching your goal)
    Summary: A biography of bodybuilder and movie star,
Arnold Schwarzenegger.
    ISBN 0-86593-260-3
    1. Schwarzenegger, Arnold—Juvenile literature.
2. Bodybuilders—United States—Biography—Juvenile
literature. 3. Motion picture actors and actresses—United
States—Biography—Juvenile literature.
[1. Schwarzenegger, Arnold. 2. Bodybuilders. 3. Actors and
actresses.] I. Title. II. Series.
GV545.52.S38M44 1993
646.75'092—dc20
[B]   92-42288
                                                                CIP
                                                                 AC

I'm your brother," said big, strong Arnold Schwarzenegger. He was talking to a very short person in a movie called Twins. The idea that two such different men were brothers was funny. Where did this man of muscle get his sense of humor?

Arnold did not have a childhood full of laughter. He was born on July 30, 1947, in a small town in Austria. Austria is a country in Europe. Aurelia and Gustav Schwarzenegger raised their two sons in a town called Thal.

The family did not have much money. Their house had no bathrooms. They did not have a water faucet in the kitchen. There was no telephone or a refrigerator.

"With that kind of upbringing, you don't take anything for granted," said Arnold.

Arnold learned to run fast and play physical games. He did these things rather than play with toys. His mother made sure her sons followed a regular routine. His father was strict and made Arnold and his brother exercise every morning.

"We had squats and situps fifteen minutes before breakfast," said Arnold. When the boys made mistakes they were punished. Arnold remembers that they were punished often.

Arnold loved to go see adventure movies with strong heroes. If he liked a movie he would see it many times. Arnold dreamed about being a powerful and important person. He also became curious about America.

"I was meant for something big," Arnold thought. He didn't want to stay in a "little country."

At thirteen he started exercising hard to become bigger and stronger. He began lifting weights. He pushed them with his legs as well as his arms. His parents disapproved. They thought "working out" was strange. But Arnold trained for at least five hours a day.

Arnold joined the Austrian army. His body grew stronger because he had more meat to eat than ever before. He wanted to be a champion bodybuilder. After just one month he won a contest in Germany. His army unit was proud of him.

He grew so strong he could lift 500 pounds. Arnold focused all his effort on making his muscles big. When he was just 20 years old, he became the youngest man to win the Mr. Universe title. He also won a weightlifting championship.

Arnold came to America in 1968 to write about bodybuilding and to compete. In 1970, he won three prizes. They were the Mr. World, Mr. Universe, and Mr. Olympia titles. No one had ever done this before. He was nicknamed "the Austrian Oak." In five more years he had won dozens of bodybuilding titles.

Arnold won prizes with his strong body, but he also went to college. He studied business. He saved the money he earned from bodybuilding and bought buildings and land. He prospered. He also became an American citizen in 1983.

The Austrian Oak was now a famous man. He told people how important it was to exercise and be healthy. He wrote three books on bodybuilding. Bodybuilding was now more popular because of Arnold.

Arnold had his dream of being a world champion. He looked for a new challenge. Something still bigger. Movies.

He appeared in a movie about bodybuilding called *Stay Hungry*. Arnold knew that to reach his next goal he had to really want it. It was like being hungry for food. Arnold had to stay hungry to be an actor.

Arnold was in a movie called *Pumping Iron*. People saw that he had a lot of personality. But he wanted to be in more movies. People told him he could not. He had a funny accent and he was just a bodybuilder. "That won't stop me," he said.

He studied acting and improved his speech. He put the same energy into learning English as he did in muscle building. Would audiences make fun of the Austrian bodybuilder?

In 1982, *Conan the Barbarian* made millions of dollars with Arnold as the star. Later he made *The Terminator* and *Terminator II*. These were exciting action movies. People saw that Arnold was a good actor. Then he made the comedy *Twins* and made audiences laugh.

Arnold was now a movie star.

In 1986, Arnold married Maria Shriver. She was well known as a television reporter. She was also the niece of President John F. Kennedy.

One day President George Bush asked Arnold to be chairman of the President's Council on Physical Fitness. He went from movie star to a national symbol of health.

Today more men, women and children are going to gyms and working out to stay fit. Physical fitness has become more popular. Arnold is glad.

Arnold says he does not think about his success much. "I just go on. You have to always make up a new goal. Always stay hungry."

Reaching Your Goal

What do you want to do? Do you want to be an astronaut? A cook? If you want something you must first set goals. Here are some steps to help you reach them.

1. Explore Your Goals

Asking questions can help you decide if reaching your goal is what you really want.

Will I be happier if I reach this goal?

Will I be healthier if I reach this goal?

2. Name Your Goals

It is harder to choose a goal if it is too general.

Do you want to be "happy?"

Learn to blow up a balloon.

Learn to ride a two-wheel bicycle.

Finish a book a week.

Name the goals you want to reach.

3. Start Small

Try reaching your goal with smaller goals.
Do you want to learn to skateboard?
Try standing on it first without moving.
Do you want to build a dollhouse?
Have an adult show you how to use tools.

4. Small Goals Turn Into Big Ones

Learning to improve your spelling can be
a goal.
Practice shorter words first.
Learn to use bigger words in sentences.
Enter a spelling bee.

5. Stick With It

People like Arnold Schwarzenegger reached
their goals by working hard. They didn't let
others talk them out of their goals. You can do
it too!

Reaching Your Goal Books

Jim Abbott Left-handed Wonder

Hans Christian Andersen A Fairy Tale Life

Cher Singer and Actress

Chris Burke He Overcame Down Syndrome

Henry Cisneros A Hard Working Mayor

Beverly Cleary She Makes Reading Fun

Bill Cosby Superstar

Roald Dahl Kids Love His Stories

Jane Goodall The Chimpanzee's Friend

Jim Henson Creator of the Muppets

Jesse Jackson A Rainbow Leader

Michael Jordan A Team Player

Ted Kennedy, Jr. A Lifetime of Challenges

Jackie Joyner-Kersee Track-and-Field Star

Ray Kroc Famous Restaurant Owner

Christa McAuliffe Reaching for the Stars

Dale Murphy Baseball's Gentle Giant

Charles Schulz Great Cartoonist

Arnold Schwarzenegger Hard Work Brought Success

Dr. Seuss We Love You

Samantha Smith Young Ambassador

Steven Spielberg He Makes Great Movies

The Rourke Corporation, Inc.
P.O. Box 3328
Vero Beach, FL 32964